MW00366333

WORD ON THE STREET

"All cultures are rooted in beliefs. In *Leadership That Rocks*, Jim Knight unleashes the greatest belief of all: the belief in one's self. Readers will be inspired to unleash the power they hold inside themselves and affect changes they thought impossible in the culture of their organizations."

Don Fox, CEO, Firehouse Subs

"Jim Knight is once again the rock star of creating a thriving business culture. In his follow-up book *Leadership That Rocks*, the author builds on his stellar accomplishment in *Culture That Rocks* by focusing on the role leaders play in creating a culture that exceeds expectations and indeed rates an eleven!"

Elizabeth McCormick, motivational leadership speaker and former U.S. Army Black Hawk pilot

"Jim Knight has a very unique viewpoint on leadership, influenced by a rock-and-roll flair. I'm excited for the future generation of leadership that Jim is creating. You *need* to read this book."

Jeremy Ryan Slate, entrepreneur and top 100 podcaster, *Create Your Own Life*

"Jim Knight has done a masterful job outlining the critical elements of personal leadership required today to truly transform an organization's culture. Full of real-world examples and meaty takeaways, *Leadership That Rocks* moves the needle from a strategy-based approach to a culture-driven roadmap to success. Every new leader should have this book on their bookshelf."
Steve Cockram, co-founder, GiANT Worldwide

"In *Leadership That Rocks*, Jim Knight shows us that successful leadership, rock star company culture and consistently great business results are all intertwined. Real-world stories + inspiring insights = the perfect leadership playlist. Take a radical leap, buy this book and amp your success up to eleven!"
Steve Farber, founder, The Extreme Leadership Institute; author of *The Radical Leap* and *Love Is Just Damn Good Business*

LEADERSHIP
THAT
ROCKS

1 CULTURE THAT ROCKS

LEADERSHIP

JIM KNIGHT

TAKE YOUR
BRAND'S CULTURE
TO ELEVEN AND
AMP UP RESULTS

THAT
ROCKS

PAGE TWO BOOKS

Cataloguing in publication information
is available from Library and Archives Canada.
ISBN 978-1-77458-066-0 (paperback)
ISBN 978-1-77458-067-7 (ebook)

Page Two
pagetwo.com

Edited by Kendra Ward
Copyedited by Tilman Lewis
Cover and interior design by Peter Cocking

LeadershipThatRocksBook.com
KnightSpeaker.com

For Theo Menswar—a true inspiration to us all

SET LIST

SOUND
CHECK

I COULD HAVE looked at it either way: as a really crappy situation or as a fantastic challenge.

I chose the latter.

Circumstances be damned! No person or obstacle was going to deter me from my path. This included my unsupportive boss who, despite working in a vibrant and amazing company culture, did not share the same value orientation as the brand. I absolutely loved the business. But here I was, a new manager with a world-class company, and my immediate supervisor was my biggest obstacle to cultural nirvana.

Have you been in a situation like this? Where one leader is the sole cog in the wheel preventing the company's culture or your career from positively moving forward?

Ugh. It's so frustrating.

And all too common.

YOU CAN BE THE CATALYST THAT SPARKS A CULTURAL FLAME

———

For some context, I had been working at Hard Rock Cafe as a host. I loved every moment of it. And because I had a background in teaching and (humble brag) a strong work ethic that included passion and commitment, I was quickly promoted from host to staff trainer to new-store-opening trainer for the multinational chain. Then, while I was on a trip to open a new restaurant, I was promoted to manager. As part of that transition, the corporate headquarters created a unique position for me: corporate training manager. I was to be based in my home location to run manager shifts and automatically pulled away for any new store openings as a manager/host trainer combo. This was the best of both worlds. I developed leadership skills in one location while the company paid me to travel the world and impact others who were new to the brand. It was awesome.

But my boss hated it.

The general manager was a nice enough guy, but he was not keen on the idea of a manager who he did not personally hire coming and going at the discretion of the company's corporate office. And so, he gave me no employee department to oversee. He did not invite me to attend the weekly manager meetings. He scheduled me all night shifts, on the most undesirable days of the week—a position commonly referred to in the industry as the "PM GM." The only real business responsibilities he assigned to me were the ones nobody else wanted: food safety and sanitation. Not the sexiest of business areas.

When he carved me out of his leadership team, I had a choice, one that swung from "rage against the machine" to "should I stay or should I go?" But anger and giving up are not part of my DNA.

As former Xerox chair and CEO Ursula Burns famously said: "Where you are is not who you are." I would not be defined by a singular moment in time imposed on me by someone else, even if that someone was my boss. Instead, I chose to make my manager's negative actions irrelevant—to me and to the culture I wanted to preserve. I chose to create a *culture that rocks* every time I walked into the building. I decided to become for others the leader that I always wanted in a manager.

I aspired to be the leader that my team wanted and that the brand deserved.

In lieu of the direct leadership and support of my manager, I created and perpetuated a culture that rocked on my own. And because of that mindset, I became a culture catalyst. And so can you. You don't need anyone's permission to have a great time in a leadership role or to strengthen the company's culture when your heart and mind are in the right place.

I hope you never experience a situation where you are not supported by your direct supervisor, but whatever your circumstance, you absolutely have the power to be a *leader that rocks*. You can be the catalyst that sparks a cultural flame. And I can help.

Let's start the fire.

"If everything was
perfect, you would
never learn and you
would never grow."

BEYONCÉ

SETTING THE STAGE

NO DOUBT the two decades I spent working at Hard Rock helped shape who I am today and my philosophies. But my time in hospitality is only a partial set list of the strategies that I now share with organizations and individuals around the world.

Actually, acquiring a music degree in college, spending six years as a substitute middle school teacher and working in restaurants for almost thirty years all influence my career today. I still pull the levers of those industries, turning the experiences I gained from each as stepping-stone tenets to live and work by and to share with others. In the years since I "retired from corporate life," I've had the great fortune of giving keynote speeches to fantastic organizations in many different industries and countries, I've studied and spent time with amazing leaders who have taken their brands to iconic heights, and I've written a bestselling book on the topic of company culture.

After years of delivering thousands of keynote speeches on various subjects, I started to notice a trend in the questions that would follow each session. Inevitably attendees would ask:

- "What other topics do you talk about?"
- "Can you do this speech for my company?"
- "Do you do any consulting?"
- "What kind of hair care products do you use?" (Actually, this was often the first question.)

However, one of the most common questions after I give a speech on organizational culture comes from new or middle managers: "How can I enhance my company's culture when I have no direct reports and I'm not an executive?"

Of course, every person in a company contributes to its culture, but sometimes it takes a little extra explanation to persuade junior leaders that they do indeed have the ability to "amp up" their environment. In fact, this question is one of the main reasons I wrote *Leadership That Rocks*. I want leaders at any level, in any industry, to have the strategies to create a culture that professionals dream about every day.

As environmental activist Greta Thunberg says: "You are never too small to make a difference."

To be fair, she was talking about everyone's personal responsibility for saving the planet. But her sentiment works perfectly for any level of leadership affecting a company's culture. You absolutely *can* make a difference.

CULTURE THAT ROCKS

In my first book, *Culture That Rocks*, I laid out a holistic leadership approach to enhancing a brand. But like trying to explain the meaning of life, the definition of love, the secrets of the universe or the ending of *Lost*, you can only provide so much information in one place and still produce an interesting, coherent resource. That first book covers a lot of ground, touching on many facets of organizational culture: hiring and retaining top talent, fostering a diverse workforce, delivering stellar customer service, recognizing the type of leadership required to make it all happen, enhancing communication, supporting philanthropy, adopting technology, creating compelling branding and more. Those concepts are like popular hit songs in a longer playlist of company culture, each with an arc I explore further in this new Culture That Rocks series.

Leadership That Rocks is the first book in the series. It seems appropriate to start with leadership, because of how critical it is in creating, maintaining or revolutionizing a company's culture. So, although you will hear a lot about company culture, this *is* a leadership book. It includes ideas, stories and best practices for *how* to strengthen the culture. This book also lays the groundwork for the others in the series:

Each book is a targeted, robust resource addressing specific needs. If you collect the series, you will be investing in a detailed blueprint for taking your company's culture to legendary, sustainable heights.

And that will just make you rock even harder.

DO THE WORK

The real impact will come when you put in the work of studying and implementing my suggestions. In the learning and development world, there is a big difference between just watching a video and taking an e-learning course, where the interactivity creates much more stickiness. I'm an educator at heart; my hope is that you retain and actively implement the ideas I share with you so that you can create a best-in-class culture.

At the end of each chapter of this book, I provide an at-a-glance review of its most impactful points. Consider these the main lyrics of the overall tune, so that you don't get lost in the melody and the beat. In addition to this low-hanging fruit, in the "Encore" at the end of this book is a list of action items that you can immediately do to enhance your leadership and ignite your brand's cultural revolution.

You can also download a free companion workbook of tough questions and meaningful activities at

LeadershipThatRocksBook.com, if you want to dive deeper into the process—whether as a personal assessment, as a playbook to implement immediate change or perhaps as a collective work project with your team.

THE PERFECT SOUNDTRACK

When you purchased this book, you invested in the future. The future of your career, the future of your business and the future of an integral piece of your company's identity—its culture. Through thick and thin, good times and bad, a business thrives and flourishes based on the strength and authenticity of its culture. Companies with strong, anchored cultures will grow and prosper, while those with weak, frail cultures will wilt and eventually die.

But here's one unquestionable truth bomb: The greatest accelerant to a cultural flame is leadership.

THE GREATEST ACCELERANT TO A CULTURAL FLAME IS LEADERSHIP.

——

In the pages ahead, I define what organizational culture is, highlight its role in a business' success and weave through bold philosophies like becoming a "culture-driven leader" and a "catalyst for change." I provide specific examples and suggestions every step of the way. Some of the ideas may be too lofty for you to attempt right away, while others are no-brainers that can be implemented tomorrow with immediate results. Either way, *Leadership That Rocks* will stack your playlist with rock-solid tunes to create the perfect soundtrack for your brand. Congratulations!

And buckle up.

Being a leader on a quest to amp up your company's culture might be one of the hardest things you will ever do, but the journey is so worth it. It can be life-changing.

Like being at your first rock concert—it's unforgettable.

GREATEST HIT

1. **You can make a difference**—no matter where you are in your company or career, there is always opportunity to lead in a way that will take your brand's culture to eleven.

"To create something from nothing is one of the greatest feelings; and I wish it upon everybody. It's heaven."

PRINCE

CULTURE-DRIVEN LEADERS

MANY COMPANIES ignore organizational culture. It's not important to them. For decades, business leaders have been conditioned to focus exclusively on strategy and operations, with the hope that a strong culture will eventually be developed once they attain some success. It's totally understandable... and completely wrong.

As serial entrepreneur, bestselling author and media mogul Gary Vaynerchuk (or "Gary V" to his fans) famously said: "Company culture is the backbone of any successful organization."

The reason leaders of great brands focus on organizational culture first and foremost is to drive a business' ultimate success. Focusing exclusively on tactical nuts and bolts will keep a company from becoming legendary—and companies that succumb to this small-time thinking will wallow in a malaise, constantly pushing the strategy-of-the-day to attain financial success.

Rock star leaders understand the difference between the two approaches and seek a higher purpose. They opt for the long-term sustainability of culture versus the limited focus of an annual strategy. Tony Hsieh, the late, iconic founder of Zappos, put it this way: "If you get the culture right, most of the other stuff will just take care of itself."

Hsieh was so right. Unlike processes, tools, products and strategies, all of which can be easily copied, culture is unique. So unique, in some cases, that replicating it is too hard for competitors to even attempt. And that's the advantage. A great organizational culture provides differentiation for consumers and employees alike. It should be hard to copy. But it shouldn't be hard to understand. Yet so many leaders ignore culture because they don't understand it. So, that's where we need to start— understanding what culture is.

CULTURE DEFINED

Some say that culture is *everything*, while others insist it is only the company's outwardly visible characteristics. Claiming that organizational culture is too broad to define, many won't even try. Then they wonder why their explanation of it—and its very existence—is fuzzy. Although I'm in the "culture is everything" camp and see proof of it in every facet of a brand, I have come to believe that all roads lead back to human behavior.

I define an organization's culture as simply "a collection of individual behaviors." That's it. That's the purest and easiest definition I can think of to communicate what a brand's culture is. Essentially, culture is inherent in the behaviors of a company's employees. All organizational practices and the results produced—positive and negative—exist only because individuals *make* them happen. Which makes deciding who joins the band imperative to the culture.

Now and forever, culture is only as strong or as weak as the employees that make up the organization.

Some thought leaders would like you to believe that culture is defined by a set of behaviors that remain unchanged over time—but that's wrong. Behaviors *do* change, because people change—they come and go in a company all the time. Culture change is inevitable. What you want is the *right* culture change.

Surround yourself with the right people, and you'll have the right culture.

ATTAINING ROCK STAR STATUS

During tough economic times—like the gas prices and inflation of the 70s in the U.S., the financial collapse of 2008 or the global pandemic in 2020, when uncertainty and fear run rampant throughout the business community—everyone scrambles to be seen as the best choice in their competitive set. Some brands focus on a single strategy, while others desperately attack anything and everything to survive or at least distance themselves from the rest. But everyone seeks the limelight. All business leaders want their company to come out on top, regardless of the economic environment.

SURROUND YOURSELF WITH THE RIGHT PEOPLE, AND YOU'LL HAVE THE RIGHT CULTURE.

———

Most leaders are on a perpetual quest to get their brand to number one. But to do that, in many cases, they're going to have to change some things about the company. They have to commit to enhancing their company's culture versus engaging in product-oriented or market-driven strategies. This might mean subtle changes for some organizations; others may need a drastic overhaul. Why make these changes? Because at the end of the day, a company's culture contributes an enormous amount to its success. In fact, many trusted thought leaders believe it is *the* contributing factor to a business' sustained success.

Joe Maddon | Chicago Cubs

Joe Maddon is a Major League Baseball manager who helmed several teams during his career, none more famous than his winning run with the Chicago Cubs. Before Maddon took the reins in 2015, the Cubs had ended their previous three seasons in last place in their division, which only solidified the team's decades-old moniker, "the lovable losers." The system that Maddon inherited was mired in heritage, process and analytics—the backbone of most MLB clubs. But Maddon knew that he was leading unique people who required the perfect balance of guidance and flexibility.

Starting on day one, Maddon shifted the organization from strategy-based to cultural. He changed the environment by implementing a healthy dose of fun, non-traditional management practices. His wacky motivational tactics included encouraging dance-offs in the pitchers' bullpen, blaring classic rock during field practices, commissioning paintings with customized messages and hanging them throughout the clubhouse, inviting a magician into the locker room to pass on a little magic to the team, launching impromptu karaoke sessions and encouraging players to wear cartoon character footie pajamas on long flights home after a road game for maximum comfort.

Sure, Maddon had a deep knowledge of baseball, but with his focus on individual personalities and his infectious positivity, he led the Chicago Cubs to victory in 2016's World Series, the team's first championship in 108 years.

Joe Maddon is a culture-driven leader.

CULTURE IS LIKE O$_2$

Regardless of industry, an organization's culture is its lifeblood. That culture, when strong and vibrant, pumps through the veins of the masses and guides, inspires and motivates each person to rise to the challenges. When a culture is unknown, uncertain or even unbearable, a company's lifeblood may be so deficient that the organization becomes anemic. As a result, people lose interest. Poor decisions are common. Employee performance weakens. Results skew. The culture inevitably dies. In this downward spiral, the business relies on individuals to survive, but those same valuable assets cannot identify with the current state of the company's culture and therefore are not motivated to contribute.

Ignoring the cultural health of the business is like failing to clean a fish tank, allowing the water to get dirty and the green algae to take over, leaving the fish gasping for air. Culture is like oxygen.

In fact, strong cultures are to organizations what life-giving oxygen is to the body, while weak ones are like poisonous carbon monoxide.

See if you agree with the brands that, in my opinion, are pumping oxygen through their organizational veins:

AMAZON APPLE BUC-EE'S CHICK-FIL-A
CINNABON COCA-COLA COSTCO WHOLESALE
DELTA AIR LINES DICK'S SPORTING GOODS
FEDEX FIRST WATCH GEEK SQUAD GOOGLE
HARLEY-DAVIDSON IKEA IN-N-OUT BURGER
KIMPTON HOTELS & RESTAURANTS LEGO
MARVEL STUDIOS MOD PIZZA NETFLIX
NIKE OPRAH WINFREY PATAGONIA
PELOTON PIXAR PUBLIX SUPER MARKETS
RAISING CANE'S CHICKEN FINGERS
RED BULL RITZ-CARLTON SALESFORCE
SHEETZ SOUTHWEST AIRLINES SPACEX
ST. JUDE CHILDREN'S RESEARCH HOSPITAL
STARBUCKS TAYLOR SWIFT ULTA BEAUTY
TOMS WEGMANS FOOD MARKETS ZAPPOS
THE CONTAINER STORE VICTORIA'S SECRET
VIRGIN WALT DISNEY WORLD WAWA
WHOLE FOODS MARKET

You are likely familiar with most of these brands—and for good reason. They are all wildly successful. Many of them are Fortune 500 businesses or recipients of awards like Best Companies to Work For—and their leaders could also write books about how to create a strong, positive culture. They have a track record of building culture that resonates not only with their employees, but also with the public, on a widespread, even global, level.

Imagine walking into the headquarters of Google, Zappos, Starbucks or any of these great companies. What would it look like? What would it feel like? What would you hear? What would you observe about the employees? My guess is that you already have a preconceived, positive idea about such an experience. This is, in part, because of the public-facing culture that the leaders of these companies have created. They want you to identify their names and products with strong culture because it will eventually sell their products and services. The evidence is clear in the totality of a company's business outcomes and eventual lifespan: culture matters.

Just ask Gary V or Joe Maddon.

LEADERSHIP SELF-AWARENESS

Are you in a culture-driven organization that is pumping oxygen?

Take a moment to "climb under the hood of the car" to see whether your organization is in good repair—perhaps just needing an oil change or minor tune-up—or if its engine is in need of a serious cultural overhaul. To help, I have collated a list of questions for you to ponder or work through with your team. The brand's personality will become glaringly apparent when you honestly answer questions like these:

- What are the observable characteristics that make up your company's culture?

- How is your company's culture taught (video, instructor-led classroom, wallet cards, posters, print manuals, storytelling, social media and so on)?

- What positive business results can you point to as resulting from your company's strong brand culture?

- What characteristics do you think your team would say make up the culture?

- What characteristics do you think your customers would say make up the culture?

- Does your company's executive team refer to the brand's culture in discussions and important decisions?

These are only thought-starters; they are, in fact, just a partial list of the questions included in my  free Culture Assessment, which you can access at CultureThatRocks.com (look under Merch on the home page). Feel free to download, distribute and discuss the questions with your team to develop an organic, collaborative self-assessment of your business. At least, it will give you a baseline from which you can plan a process for creating, maintaining or altering your company's culture.

Do the work, reap the rewards.

GREATEST HITS

1. **Become a culture-driven leader**—whatever your level of leadership, use your influence to move the company from strategy-based to culture-focused.

2. **Focus on hiring top talent**—surround yourself with "rock stars" to get world-class results.

3. **Constantly self-assess**—regularly challenge yourself and the team on your leadership and the health of the business.

"Fame or perceived success—it all comes from group think."

CHANCE THE RAPPER

ROCK BANDS
& BUSINESS
BRANDS

E VEN THOUGH "culture" is a nebulous, unseen principle—hard to prove and harder still to measure—people know it exists. But if you can't nail down a coherent definition of culture, you won't be able to easily create, adjust or protect it.

Ask any five people what "corporate culture" is and you are likely to get five different answers, some specific, some vague. And it's possible that all of them would be right. Here's the dilemma: If some people in an organization have a positive, definitive view of its culture while others are clueless about it, there will be widespread confusion about the company's direction and possibly even its desired business outcomes.

That's why I give culture the universal definition of "a collection of individual behaviors."

The desired behaviors will produce the desired culture.

COLLECTIVE SOUP

Most organizational experts will say that a company's mission, vision, values, rituals, traditions, beliefs, customs, standards, methodology and jargon all combine to create an environment over time. This environment impacts how team members interact with one another and their customers—and, ultimately, the overall performance of the business. This collective soup of characteristics creates the almost human-like personality of a culture.

Rock bands are like that too.

CULT OF PERSONALITY

Consider the "cultures" of three generational touring artists: the Grateful Dead, Jimmy Buffett and the Dave Matthews Band. Ask any Dead Head, Parrot Head or DMB fan if these artists have a culture and the resounding answer will be yes. Perhaps they won't pinpoint the exact characteristics that make these bands a living personality—although some fans will happily rattle off several—but people know a thriving culture when they experience it.

The same can be said for arena-level musicians like The Rolling Stones, Taylor Swift, Garth Brooks, BTS, Lady Gaga, Black Eyed Peas, Ariana Grande, Metallica, Wu-Tang Clan, P!nk and Imagine Dragons. These acts pride themselves on creating such mind-blowing and immersive events that concerts become cultural experiences layering onto the artists' personas.

There are many similarities between the music world and business. A lot of qualities collectively develop your business' personality, whether those are team dynamics, collaboration, overcoming challenges, work-life balance, innovation, producing desired products, surprising the audience or creating sustainable results.

ALIVE ON THE INSIDE

A company's culture is the brand's personality. It's a living organism—like a culture in a petri dish, where people are the micro-organisms. See where I'm going here? The brand's personality changes as different "micro-organisms" affect it. Each person comes to the table with their own personal culture shifts and their own learned behaviors, and the culture of any organization can only exist because of the people embodying it.

Famous author, brand executive and chair of the board of AARP Libby Sartain put it this way: "If a brand doesn't live on the inside, it can't thrive on the outside."

As a company both succeeds and struggles through the years, its culture becomes more profound, wielding greater influence on all the stakeholders within it to conform to organizational norms. In this perpetual cycle, employees strengthen the brand's culture, and so, define the brand's personality.

Consumers experience and come to know a company's culture because of the consistent, widely shared, collective behaviors of the internal team.

Take note: This doesn't just apply to positive organizational cultures; it is simply how a company establishes its "personality." An organization's founders and leadership may hope that their culture is positive and that it won't change over time... but it will. People come and go all the time. Just like a rock band, a culture is only as strong as the people currently employed and collectively making up the heart and soul of the organization. That's why it's up to you, as a leader, to choose your people wisely and foster the kinds of behaviors you want your customers to experience.

Colleen Barrett | Southwest Airlines

In 2010, Southwest Airlines' president emerita Colleen Barrett co-authored a book with business icon Ken Blanchard called *Lead with LUV: A Different Way to Create Real Success.* In it, she explains why it would be hard for another company to copy the airline's rock star culture—its secret sauce. She writes: "I don't dictate our Culture; none of our Officers do. Rather, it stems from the collective personality of our People. And they are what makes us the provider of choice in the airline industry."

Southwest Airlines is widely known for its great internal and external culture—so much so that *Fortune* magazine has ranked the carrier near the top of its World's Most Admired Companies survey every year since 1994. That doesn't happen by accident. Results like that are predicated on a collection of committed brand ambassadors.

An organization can adjust its processes and infrastructure to enhance the perceived culture. Like any system, however, these changes are only as effective as the human beings making them.

PAST VS. PRESENT

People often equate an organization's culture with its history. But while we all love nostalgia, history is not the same as culture, and the words "culture" and "heritage" cannot be used interchangeably.

A company's heritage is rooted in the past. Companies like Nike, Harley-Davidson and Chick-fil-A have a rich heritage complete with founding values, traditions, customs and success stories. These storytelling opportunities must be captured and shared, so that a company's lineage can thrive and the entrepreneurial spirit consistently inspires new leaders like you to become culture catalysts. You must become a "keeper of the cultural flame," helping the knowledge capital of your brand to flourish. Additionally, a company's history influences the perception of its culture, but you cannot just rely on the stories of how the brand got started, its meteoric rise or even how long it has existed to define the culture. Heritage is about the past.

Culture, on the other hand, is about the present. If the culture of a brand is its collective employee behaviors, then *that* culture is unique at any given time, depending on who is in the organization at that moment.

THE REVOLVING DOOR OF BANDMATES

Where would The Who be in our mental soundtrack if guitarist Pete Townshend were not in the band? Would Rush still be in the Rock & Roll Hall of Fame if drum god Neil Peart were never a part of that Canadian prog-rock trio? Would Beyoncé be the fierce, dominant force she is today had she not stepped away from Destiny's Child? Would One Direction have any collective success if Harry Styles was absent from the group? Would Fifth Harmony still be the global phenomenon they are if Camila Cabello had not bailed on the girl group? (Okay… forget the last example.)

Every member of the band is critical. Lose a member, add a member or replace a member and the band is forever changed. Perhaps for the better, perhaps not. The hope, of course, is that the group's evolution is positive, rewarding, successful and sustainable... but it is completely dependent on the roster.

Businesses are like that too. Every company is in flux as people come and go. The culture is ever-evolving, never stagnant. It is either getting stronger or weaker, depending on who's employed at a given time. As someone leaves, the organizational culture changes. The shift may be small, but it is a change, nonetheless. When a new team member joins the company, the culture morphs again.

Think of culture change from this systemic standpoint: As one piece of the culture leaves and another joins, the individuals that make up the culture will begin to replace one another and eventually reinvent the culture entirely. Sometimes the change happens dramatically, as when someone in a key leadership role leaves and is replaced by a new executive. Other times, change results from continuous small shifts, until it becomes fully apparent to everyone. Regardless of how quickly a company's culture changes, a revolving door of new hires guarantees that it will, inevitably, change.

ARE YOU SURROUNDED BY ROCK STARS OR LIP-SYNCHERS?

———

Heritage is important and should be captured and effectively shared, but the here-and-now is what most leaders seek to address. The present state of things—ultimately defined by individual behavior—is the actual company culture.

Employ the right brand ambassadors and you create a culture that rocks.

Envied companies like Ritz-Carlton, Sheetz and The Container Store get it. Each has made a conscious decision to focus on hiring only rock stars—the best talent possible—which is how they continue to protect their celebrated culture. And we are all better off because of that.

Even if you're a new leader or middle manager, this awesome responsibility sits squarely on your shoulders. So, ask yourself, are you surrounded by rock stars or lip-synchers?

GREATEST HITS

1. **Focus internally for external results—** positive customer experiences only happen because of the consistent, widely shared, collective behaviors of the internal team.

2. **Choose people over process—** many adjustments can be made to an organization's systems, but changes are only as effective as the human beings making them happen.

3. **Don't get stuck in the past—** celebrate the company's history (heritage), but focus primarily on the present and future (culture).

"I don't regret any of the decisions I've made in my life. Because with every choice I've made, I've learned something new."

ARIANA GRANDE

START WITH YOU

WHEN IT comes down to it, changing the culture of an organization you love will be among the most challenging responsibilities you'll face. It takes time, patience, persistence, effort, know-how and passion. But it's not impossible—and it's completely worthwhile.

Like most things in life that require an overhaul, culture change starts on the inside. I'm not just referring to the "below the surface" processes of the company. I'm talking about something even more internal. Culture shifts start with each one of us.

They start with *you*.

PERSONAL CULTURE SHIFTS

Going back to when I was a young boy, I can point to specific moments when I was on a clear path of my choosing, only to have my world rocked, hurling me in a different direction. Early on, I wanted to be a fireman

CULTURE CHANGE STARTS ON THE INSIDE

___

or a paramedic like my father—until we rolled up to a traffic accident and I witnessed the horror of it. My father saved lives, but the trauma was too much for me. That moment steered me away from that profession. I also wanted to play organized football... until the day in high school that I put on the uniform and went to practice. I was hit so hard that the air was knocked out of me. That instant changed my mind about playing the sport. Another life-changing moment occurred in college, where I studied music and hoped to become a professional musician. I soon discovered that to make a living in that field, you had to be really good. I was adequate, but not great. This realization again altered my professional direction.

I call these moments "personal culture shifts." They are inflection points—defining moments in a person's life, each one contributing to that person's identity. My personal culture shifts may have been uncomfortable and full of uncertainty at the time, but they also helped shape my internal, personal culture and made me who I am today. As an executive at a globally recognized music and hospitality brand for more than twenty years and an entrepreneurial keynote speaker for another ten, I'm convinced those personal inflection points have now positively influenced hundreds of organizational cultures.

We all go through personal culture shifts. Whether these events are considered positive or negative at the time, they can all be learning experiences. Some people will look at these moments as things that happen *to* them, while others will look at them as things that happen *for* them.

Rachel Hollis, a lifestyle blogger and motivational speaker, writes about this concept in her bestselling book *Girl, Wash Your Face*: "What if the hard stuff, the amazing stuff, the love, the joy, the hope, the fear, the weird stuff, the funny stuff, the stuff that takes you so low you're lying on the floor crying and thinking, How did I get here?... What if none of it is happening *to* you? What if all of it is happening *for* you?"

This is a mindset, really. Some people look at life positively and think that every experience happens for a reason and that those moments are part of life's discovery; they are open to the journey and where life takes them. Other people have more of a victim mentality and look at these personal inflection points as negative. They believe life's experiences randomly impose changes on their life's plan. These people are rarely prepared for change; they tend to feel as though their world is caving in around them rather than stay open to new possibilities.

Which of these mindsets best describes your disposition? Are life's challenges leading you down a "highway to hell" or are they steps on the "stairway to heaven"? Because mindset matters.

Embracing experiences as opportunities allows us to bring fresh perspectives to the party. And that can be incredibly empowering.

Felicia White | Church's Chicken

Early in Felicia White's career at Church's Chicken as a mid-level manager (national field trainer), she received less-than-stellar feedback on her communication skills during her performance appraisal from a new, outside-hire executive. Although Felicia was widely considered a rock star at the company, was crushing her responsibilities and was the "go-to" resource for her peers, her boss' explanation of the sole below-target rating was: "People do not know you." His point was that Felicia's team members craved to be brought into her thought processes and ideas to ultimately be inspired and motivated to produce sustainable results. Unbeknownst to Felicia at the time, her boss was pushing her to transition from a great manager of tasks to an iconic leader of people.

Felicia could have taken this stimulus negatively, but instead she accepted it as an opportunity. This mindset set the stage for Felicia's historic rise at Church's. Her personal culture shift inspired her to start thinking more strategically—about her communication and how to better affect the overall brand. With a sense of urgency, Felicia:

- became more vocal with her team, sharing her vision and ideas early in the process;

- sought out development by attending industry associations and then shared the learnings upon returning;

- created internal mentorship and networking programs, like Church's Women's Forum;

- learned to effectively manage her boss; and

- brought her authentic self to the job.

When asked how she would advise new managers to deal with the type of "tough love" feedback that she'd received early in her leadership career, Felicia said: "When you start a car trip, you enter an address in the GPS. Obstacles (feedback) may arise, and you may be given an alternate route, but the destination never changes. The destination should *always* be the focus."

Things did not happen *to* Felicia White, they happened *for* her. And because of that mentality, she was promoted four times and is now the first vice president of global operations training and development in the company's history.

Felicia White now rocks *all* of Church's Chicken.

Ed Stack | Dick's Sporting Goods

Dick's Sporting Goods' chair and CEO, Ed Stack, took over the business from his father at age twenty-nine, propelling the brand from two stores to over eight hundred, solidifying the company as *the* place communities go for all their sporting equipment needs. In his first book, *It's How We Play the Game*, Stack shows how businesses don't always move in a straight line—and neither do their leaders. He openly details several personal culture shifts he went through as Dick's both excelled and struggled.

Ed Stack writes about the company's close call with bankruptcy from expanding too quickly without the right processes in place to manage the growth, before pulling back and reassessing their growth plans. He details his push to support youth participation in sports after noticing its dramatic decrease over several decades, because of U.S. school budget cuts nationwide and the lack of other organized sports opportunities. This became the impetus for the company's Sports Matter program, which developed local Little League baseball programs and sponsorships, provided community grant programs for high-poverty schools and partnered with sports crowdfunding organizations to help programs and coaches direct how funds raised are spent. But Stack's biggest shift to date is his decision to stop selling military assault–style rifles at Dick's Sporting Goods, offending thousands of avid hunters and loyal customers.

As Ed Stack states in his book, he grew up around guns and still believes that any American over the age of twenty-one has the right to own one. He also strongly believes that companies are responsible to the communities they serve—just as much as to the bottom line. He knew that this personal culture shift would affect the brand's short-term financial health,

ARE YOU MADLY IN LOVE WITH YOUR BRAND?

—

and that the company would not survive long term if the community it served did not. After a series of shootings in public schools, Stack's deeply held value system trumped the guaranteed revenue loss and ire that was sure to come... and he made the tough call.

Ed Stack is now considered one of the leading voices in stronger gun control measures.

Whether you agree with his decision or not, the point is that a leader's personal culture *can* shift. Things didn't happen *to* Ed Stack, they happened *for* him. He looked at the facts, assessed the situation, adjusted his approach and took a stand for what he valued. His company's culture change started with his own shift.

DEVELOP A LOVE AFFAIR

As an independent culture catalyst in a leadership role, you can build a striking relationship with your team and become a fire-starter for great change. The old adage "do what you love and love what you do" is so relevant, but the only way this happens is if your head and heart align with your organization.

Perhaps your first few jobs simply served some basic needs: shopping at the mall, going to the movies, downloading music. But once you turned your attention to a career and stepped into a leadership role, you experienced a huge personal culture shift. Your mission changed. The quest grew bigger than just making the donuts... although watching hot Krispy Kreme donuts come off the conveyor belt does sound pretty sweet.

There's no doubt in my mind that you want to make sure that your job—where you spend the majority of your waking life—is rewarding and contributes to your personal mission. So, here's my question: Are you madly in love with your brand?

It's a simple question, but if you are not 100 percent aligned with your company's purpose, mission and values, then the answer won't be as easy. In fact, it could be uncomfortable.

If you are not completely gaga about the company, then why are you there?

Is this your first time in a leadership role and you need the experience? If so, that's cool... for now.

Are the pay and benefits just too good to pass up? That's fine too... for now.

Do you like the leadership role itself, but you don't really agree with the company's positions or its values? Well, then... ugh. What are doing wasting your life there?

Listen, you don't have to agree with *every* business practice, system and tool. But when it comes to the fundamental reason for the company's existence, its guiding non-negotiables and its organizational pillars, those *must* be aligned with your personal values. Or else, at some point, you are going to have a massive reckoning with your soul.

This alignment between your individual values and the company's identity is key to your personal fulfillment and your effective participation in the brand's future. But, if you relish the leadership role you're in, for a company that you truly love, all while acknowledging that it needs a bit of a cultural revolution... then a deep emotional connection with the brand will make you a catalyst for change.

GREATEST HITS

1. **Put in the work**—sustainable culture change takes time, patience, persistence, effort, know-how and passion, but it's not impossible and it's completely worthwhile.

2. **Embrace personal culture shifts**—look at every experience as something that happens *for* you, not *to* you.

3. **Love your brand**—commit to growing with a company that has a value orientation aligned with yours.

"As a rock star, I have two instincts: I want to have fun, and I want to change the world. I have a chance to do both."

BONO

BE THE
CATALYST
FOR CHANGE

'VE ALWAYS admired people who are loyal to an organization for a long time—individuals who have watched their ideas come to life, take flight and even grow into organizational norms. These brand ambassadors dig in to move mountains and shift cultural identities. They don't just ride the back of the organization for their own interests; with the passion and commitment they put into the business' success, they earn the right to represent the company culture. Partly because of tenure, but mostly because of dedication and fearlessness, they attain the status of "culture catalyst" and the implied permission to influence the organization.

To shift the cultural pillars of a company, someone's got to be the catalyst—the change agent. Let's look at how you do that.

LIKE-MINDED DIVERSITY

Leaders at all levels need to understand that employees are the conduit for the changes that lead to any desired results. Surrounding yourself with different yet like-minded people with a passionate mission is one way to positively affect company culture. Inspiring the individuals you supervise is important, and focusing on who you bring on to the team may be just as critical for culture change.

This is where diversity can pay big dividends.

The value of a diverse workgroup has been long touted by human resources professionals and organizational psychologists alike. They maintain that a diverse workforce fosters better, more creative solutions to problems, thereby leading to sustainable growth.

And when people join an inclusive organization, they are more likely to stay longer and commit to its mission.

When that happens, the culture becomes even stronger. Think about the diverse talent in these well-known business cultures:

- Starbucks
- Zappos
- Hard Rock Cafe
- MOD Pizza
- Harley-Davidson
- First Watch

Some of the most interesting people on the planet are found in these companies. There is no doubt to the financial success and respective industry dominance of these businesses, but many brand strategists will point to the collective diversity of a company's employee base as the true "secret sauce" to its sustained success.

If your business is dependent on people for its results, continually hiring the same type of people will almost inevitably yield the same results you've been getting. These might not be bad, but they could always be better with some fresh thinking thrown into the mix. Culture catalysts spark meaningful change by hiring diverse yet like-minded people who become a willing part of the collective mission. You can do the same with just a little laser-like focus on who you onboard.

But, you ask, what if you have no choice as to who joins the brand? Ah, that's when leadership comes into play.

Colonel Rebecca Sonkiss | United States Air Force

One of my favorite culture catalysts is Colonel Rebecca Sonkiss. I met Col. Sonkiss during a speaking engagement for the U.S. Air Force, when she was the 89th Airlift Wing Commander at Joint Base Andrews in Washington, D.C. Several military branches are stationed here, as well as the presidential aircraft, and America's top government officials fly in and out of this base.

The military is traditionally super-structured, with a regulated, top-down apparatus of command and control. I assumed that it had to be like that or the whole process of making and following orders in a split second wouldn't work, but Col. Sonkiss brought a new perspective to the job. When she took command, she discovered that everyone at the 89th Airlift Wing were hitting the mark and doing their jobs. No doubt all airmen (the generic term for personnel of all genders) were ready at a moment's notice to execute their job function. And yet, something was missing. In Rebecca Sonkiss' view, it was love, care and attention.

Whoa, I was not expecting that approach from a military leader, let alone from a deployment-hardened combat aviator.

When asked what her leadership style is, Col. Sonkiss called it "Care and Be Kind." It sounds like something you might hear in the corporate world, from a successful brand that perhaps lost its way and needs to bring in some new leadership to amp up the culture. Or even something a self-help guru would tout. But from a military base commander? The Colonel was on to something fantastic.

Take a look at some of the initiatives Col. Sonkiss implemented to move to a more culture-driven environment:

- She encouraged and empowered airmen to have quality personal time when not on duty.

- She asked about and focused on airmen's families, realizing the sacrifices the whole family makes when someone serves the country.

- She emphasized the need for better communication between all levels, in particular influencing leaders to listen more to their teams and invite diversity of thought—a vision of empowerment from the bottom up.

- She heightened the focus on "customer service"—whether in support of an aircraft maintenance technician or the President of the United States—so that needs are anticipated and obstacles eliminated, allowing the end user to execute their function with excellence.

- She empowered everyone around her to make solid decisions and still held each leader accountable—lest you think it was a free-for-all under her command.

- She supported flexibility in the methods airmen took to achieve results, as long as the leader's intent was covered, reminding me of something I heard her say: "Once you give commander's intent, then let the airmen run... They will run faster every time."

One of the things Col. Sonkiss was most proud of during her tenure at Joint Base Andrews was the creation of Special Air Missions—Foreign, or SAM Fox University, which is the internally branded, professional learning platform accessible to all airmen. As part of her focus on providing ongoing development, Col. Sonkiss discovered that there was a gap in *what* and *when* people wanted to learn, but that they definitely wanted to. Hence the formation of SAM Fox. This e-learning environment targets different learning styles, provides online and classroom courseware, includes a mix of internal and civilian content, can track each airman's progress and helps guide mentorship.

With the creation of SAM Fox University, Col. Sonkiss added a much-needed layer to a culture that already rocks in the Air Force. The universal desire to grow was already in place, but it took an innovative and supportive leader to bring that program to life. Having since been promoted to Brigadier General and assigned to the Pentagon, Col. Sonkiss provided leadership during her command that every leader could learn from.

Brigadier General Rebecca Sonkiss is a culture catalyst.

CULTURE CATALYSTS TAKE BOLD CHANCES THAT OTHERS ONLY DREAM ABOUT

——

LEADING CULTURE CATALYSTS

Culture catalysts are people who protect a company's heritage yet aren't afraid to create new sparks within a brand to stoke the cultural flames. They take chances. They take bold risks that others only dream about. They can come from any leadership level or industry. Let's look at some well-known figures who rock this description on a large scale.

Elon Musk | SpaceX

I think of Elon Musk, the billionaire founder and CEO of SpaceX, who intends for humans to get to and colonize Mars during his lifetime. The combined learnings from his other successful companies— Tesla, SolarCity, OpenAI, Neuralink and The Boring Company—are all part of Musk's vision to "change the world and help humanity." In fact, his current more earthly goals include producing sustainable energy to reduce global warming and developing a high-speed transportation system, known as the Hyperloop, based on reduced-air compression tubes.

Elon Musk is a maverick.

Lizzo | Hip-Hop Artist

I think of Melissa Viviane Jefferson, known profes-
sionally as Lizzo, who has changed the game in hip-hop.
In addition to being a fantastic singer, rapper and flutist
(yep, she plays the flute during several of her on-stage
rap performances), Lizzo has broken cultural barriers.
She has become a role model to millions of fans for
promoting body positivity. Confident, talented and
unapologetically authentic, Lizzo has already made her
mark in the genre by influencing teenagers around the
world to believe they can pursue their dreams and love
themselves at the same time, regardless of the obstacle.

Lizzo is a change agent.

José Andrés | Celebrity Chef

I think of José Andrés, the Spanish-American
restaurateur, who, in addition to running dozens of
restaurants in the U.S. and becoming a celebrity chef
through appearances on *Top Chef*, *Iron Chef America*
and Anthony Bourdain's food shows, added "philanthropist" to his resumé. In response to the 2010 Haiti
earthquake, Andrés started World Central Kitchen,
which provides delicious and healthy food to people
directly affected by disasters. Coming out of the food
industry myself, I'm so proud to see José Andrés

making and distributing food in the chaos created by a hurricane, a tornado, an earthquake, a tsunami or a global pandemic.

José Andrés is a rock star.

Mary Dillon | Ulta Beauty

I think of Mary Dillon, the CEO of Ulta Beauty, the largest U.S. beauty retailer and premier destination for cosmetics, fragrance, skin care and hair care products, and salon services. In addition to vaulting the brand to the Fortune 500 and being named to Barron's 2019 list of the World's Best CEOs, Dillon's proudest achievements go beyond skin-deep metrics. Since taking over the company's reins in 2013, she has proudly created one of the most gender-diverse workforces of any large public company; shepherded a partnership with Credo Beauty to provide guests an exclusive, clean beauty collection with unrivaled transparency about sourcing, fragrance and ingredients; and established the Ulta Beauty Charitable Foundation, which donates millions of dollars to nonprofits supporting women and their families.

The biggest part of Mary Dillon's success is in her personal humility to learn from others and authentically listen to associates. Not only have some of the best ideas come from the front line, but her "no question is off limits" discussions have created an environment where associates feel valued. Mary (as she insists on being called) understands that the positive experiences associates have at Ulta translate to a positive, enthusiastic, consumer-focused culture. Retailers and consumers alike have noticed this, big time. Through Mary's authentic leadership, Ulta Beauty truly "brings possibilities to life through the power of beauty each and every day."

Mary Dillon is a culture catalyst.

CATALYSTS AT ANY LEVEL

Industry game-changers inspire us to think big and consider how we can create some awesomeness around us. But you don't have to be a globally recognized entrepreneur, famous rapper or chief executive to be a culture catalyst.

Daniel Botero | Mastering College to Career

Before Daniel Botero became a keynote speaker, best-selling author and wildly successful career consultant with his Mastering College to Career business, he worked for PepsiCo as an entry-level sales associate immediately after graduating from my college alma mater, the University of Central Florida. (Go, Knights!)

PepsiCo modestly participated in campus job fairs to attract potential new hires during Botero's time there (which obviously worked, since he joined Pepsi), but unlike the more popular Florida State University, University of Florida and University of Georgia, UCF was not considered one of the company's core recruiting schools. However, Daniel Botero was convinced he could change the dynamic and source "right fit" alumni for the brand. And so, he volunteered to take on the recruitment at his beloved college, believing that he could do a better job at attracting and influencing rock star recruits from Central Florida to join PepsiCo.

As part of his focused approach, Botero participated in every job fair. He held information sessions throughout the campus. He mentored students. He spoke at every student organization the university allowed. If there was an event happening, Daniel was there, talking about how to get a cool gig at Pepsi. And it worked. A flood of great candidates poured out of UCF—five fantastic hires the first year—which only increased each year after. So many stellar sales associates were being hired from the University of Central Florida that Botero's regional director of human resources worked with him to create a case study for UCF to become a core school for recruitment. That designation comes with increased resources allotted from PepsiCo headquarters, such as these:

- multi-tables and increased branding at job fairs;
- catered food and drinks at info sessions;
- product giveaways at events;
- more speaking opportunities for sales associate recruiters; and
- third-party companies hired to review the influx of applications.

Because of these initiatives, the recruits being sourced at UCF were better informed about PepsiCo on the front end, and the retention rate for the brand was better on the back end. Botero's initiatives produced so many great hires that PepsiCo *had* to recruit at UCF. It was unavoidable.

A SINGLE LEADER WITH A GREAT IDEA CAN START A REVOLUTION.

—

Daniel Botero is a culture catalyst. His leadership is a perfect example of a new manager taking the initiative to positively affect the company culture. To this day, the University of Central Florida is still a core school for PepsiCo's recruitment. And all parties are better because of it.

Charge On, Daniel. Charge On.

THINKING DIFFERENTLY

For real change to occur, you've got to be the heroic individual who takes the first steps toward thinking differently, applying new ideas and fearlessly defending those decisions later.

Richard Branson, the founder and CEO of Virgin, put it this way: "If we all thought the same all the time, nothing would ever change. Every company needs mavericks."

I couldn't agree more. That is exactly what culture catalysts do. They affect change for the better. It is how dictator-led countries are overthrown, philanthropic movements are started and company cultures change.

Regardless of your level, you can be one of these mavericks: a single leader with a great idea can start a revolution.

GREATEST HITS

1. **Hire diverse but like-minded people—** an inclusive workforce engaged in a shared mission fosters better, more creative solutions to problems, leading to sustainable growth.

2. **Become a culture catalyst—**while protecting the company's heritage, take bold risks that other people only dream about or are too scared to try.

3. **Get in the game—**regardless of your leadership level, real culture change only happens by thinking differently, acting on those new ideas and fearlessly defending the decisions later.

"Once you smash the building down and you're left with
just the foundations—you
can build on top of that and
create something bigger
and better and more fitting
with the times."

LUKE SPILLER (THE STRUTS)

LAY THE
GROUNDWORK

WANTING CHANGE is one thing; making it happen isn't so easy. Whether you have joined a company that just needs an adrenaline shot or you've been hanging out in an organization that requires major surgery for its failing heart, any company can be enhanced for the better. But this requires leadership. And to be an effective leader of others, you have to lay the groundwork in yourself first.

Let's talk about how to do that for your iconic career.

RESULTS OBSESSED

When you think about the most successful business leaders that you admire, some universal characteristics likely come to mind: vision, competence, trustworthiness, appreciation, generosity. And although every great leader has a specific personality and delivery style, they share the common trait of working hard to get to where they are and being driven by making things happen. Even when others dismiss their abilities or count them out, successful leaders ignore the naysayers and "will" their success into existence. They are crystal clear about the results they want to deliver and are driven to achieve them. Hard work isn't just a means to an end—it's an obsession. That may be frowned upon in some countries and social circles, but it's the type of work ethic that produces results.

Jeremy Ryan Slate | Command Your Brand Media

Jeremy Ryan Slate, the CEO of Command Your Brand Media, helps entrepreneurs hone their message and impact thousands with the power of storytelling. When he appeared as a guest on *Thoughts That Rock*, the weekly leadership podcast I co-host with my rock star colleague, Brant Menswar, we asked Jeremy for the best advice he could give our audience. His answer: "Results will take more time and effort than you can ever imagine."

This may seem like a no-brainer, but in an era when many expect immediate gratification and guaranteed results, Slate's wisdom is a great reminder that an obsessive work ethic is a foundation of sustained success. During our conversation, he shared about many personal and professional challenges, noting that it was only through sheer will and years of perseverance that he realized any measure of success. Flat-out hard work pushed through every obstacle he faced. Today, Jeremy Ryan Slate is a top 100 podcast host of *Create Your Own Life Show*, which helps people construct life on their own terms at a world-class level and has been downloaded millions of times.

Kat Cole | Focus Brands

Kat Cole, former president and COO of Focus Brands— the private equity parent company of Auntie Anne's, Cinnabon, Carvel, Jamba, Moe's Southwest Grill and others—calls obsessive hard work the "hustle muscle." This type of blazing fast and determined work ethic is learned behavior, and like any muscle, the more you use it, the more powerful the results will be. Ongoing determination, passion, commitment, a sense of urgency and a can-do work ethic, even in the face of failure, all contribute to developing this hustle muscle. But it gets stronger when a leader faces steep odds and must think fast, create alternatives and marshal whatever resources possible to achieve a result.

Kat Cole credits her own skyrocket rise to success (from Hooters waitress to president of Cinnabon to global executive, entrepreneur and philanthropist) to the grit and attributes she developed while growing up in challenging situations, having to take on adult responsibilities early in life and being afforded global leadership opportunities by the age of nineteen. In a December 2018 *Fortune* magazine article, Cole notes: "Developing a high sense of urgency and a bias for action isn't taught in books. 'Hustle muscle' comes when leaders are literally thrown into experiences where they must utilize the resources they have to achieve their objectives. Developing this leadership strength also means that you are vulnerable to failure. How can you overcome if your efforts don't yield the results you want? Will you get back up and try again? You will... if you have 'hustle muscle'! Leaders who have the guts to do the work find themselves celebrating victory on a regular basis."

Kobe Bryant | Basketball Icon

The late, great National Basketball Association superstar Kobe Bryant had hustle muscle as well. Kobe's unparalleled work ethic and obsession to win was known to many, on and off the court, during his iconic professional basketball career. Then, after his tragic death in 2020, the whole world came to know and celebrate his relentless drive. Check out a few of the many inspiring documented stories that define a results-obsessed leader:

- In high school, Kobe used to practice from 5 to 7 a.m. before classes, and then again after school ended. Many times, after all that, he would challenge one of his teammates to a one-on-one game to 100 points.

- During Kobe's rookie year in the NBA, he practiced shooting basketballs in the dark to build muscle memory.

- In the off-season, Kobe followed a 666 workout plan, which meant practicing basketball, running and lifting weights six hours a day, six days a week for six months.

HARD WORK ISN'T JUST A MEANS TO AN END—IT'S AN OBSESSION

———

- During his time in the NBA, Kobe refused to stop practicing until after he took 400 shots at the basket, which he mentally counted in every session.

- Kobe would practice shooting the exact same mid-range, typical basketball shot for an hour straight... just to perfect his shot from *that* location.

- Even after exhausting NBA practices, Kobe would randomly select a teammate to stay later, so that he could practice new moves on them.

The best example I heard during the lead-up to Kobe Byrant's funeral was from Chicago Bulls' point guard Jay Williams, who shared a story with the media of going to a practice court several hours before a game against Kobe and the Los Angeles Lakers. Kobe was already there practicing, drenched in sweat. After an hour or so of his own practice, Jay was getting ready to leave. He noticed Bryant still practicing all-out game moves, not just typical practice shots. That night, after Kobe had scored 40 points and crushed the Chicago Bulls, Jay sheepishly asked Kobe why he was in the gym so long, earlier that day. Kobe's response: "Because I saw you come in and I wanted you to know that it doesn't matter how hard you work, I am willing to work harder than you."

Nobody worked harder than Kobe Bryant. His five NBA championship titles and number-three ranking on the all-time scoring list at the time of his death are proof of his greatness and the work ethic it took to achieve it.

Hard work through the development of hustle muscle can be your story too.

Part of a leader's groundwork is in honing work ethic.

INCREMENTAL WINS

Along with a rock-solid work ethic, you've got to be willing to lay the groundwork for your big dreams in increments. Early in my corporate career, when I went from working as a host at a single Hard Rock location to working in the brand's worldwide headquarters, I wanted to make a huge, immediate impression on the company culture. I had big ideas and plenty of drive. After some good advice and serious soul-searching, however, I decided to start small and concentrate on only those few things I could directly control. I began with my own attitude: I focused on being positive and controlling my emotions. The next "baby step" in my career evolution involved focusing on just a few staff-level training initiatives. I meticulously attacked the employee handbook and the new-hire orientation. By going after these entry-level, field-based products and programs and overhauling them to match the culture and address fundamental learning principles, I earned enough clout within the organization to move on to other company initiatives.

With a little guidance from my boss, Mike Shipley (Hard Rock's Director of Training and Development), and a whole lot of earned trust with him, I made enough headway to eventually grow my circle of influence and take on more responsibilities in the organization. By validating the "use rate" of the programs I launched and securing positive feedback on their value to frontline workers, I generated enough "wins" to be trusted with even bigger responsibilities.

Eventually, Mike allowed me to take over all staff-level training programs; a few years later, I assumed all management-level training responsibilities. Ultimately, my "job" developed into a full-blown career managing the learning and development culture of the entire organization—including Mike's responsibilities after he left the company.

All of that was only possible because of my boss' direction to start small and do a few things really well. I had to walk first, before I was able to run. Through this approach, I progressed from creating training manuals and videos to producing e-learning course-ware, facilitating a corporate university and opening new properties around the world. By the time I stepped away from the brand, I could influence the company's culture in nearly every facet of the people side of the business.

DEFEND CHANGE

As a rock star leader, you've also got to be prepared to defend organizational change.

Organizational change has to happen in every company at some point, to ensure the company's survival. It's inevitable—but it doesn't have to be unbearable. To a great extent, keen leaders at any level can anticipate change of any type, prepare for it and even influence its impact on the business. If the impending change is sufficiently discussed, meticulously plotted out and clearly communicated to all levels, then buy-in is possible—and so are results.

IF YOU HATE CHANGE, THEN YOU'RE REALLY GOING TO HATE EXTINCTION.

———

However, if a leader wants to create and impose on the brand a *desired* culture change, then an added skill is required: defending the change. Desired culture change requires the same rigor as unintended change, but this time *you* are the catalyst. That comes with its own set of issues.

Your first challenge is convincing the masses to amp up the brand. Unfortunately, most people hate change. Even if it is positive change. If you are indeed the catalyst responsible for creating and delivering organizational change, even in the spirit of building up the culture, you can expect some resistance from others in the company. To rattle the thinking of staunch resisters, I have used sobering language like this: "If you hate change, then you're really going to hate extinction. Because that is what will happen to the brand if the company never alters course to stay fresh, relevant or at the pace of society."

Regardless if you are a new leader, a mid-level manager or a seasoned veteran, defending change is one of the more challenging parts of leadership. But if you start with the behavior-based ingredients like hustle muscle and building on your wins, you will have a recipe for success.

GREATEST HITS

1. **Be obsessed about results**—combine passion, commitment and a hard work ethic with thinking fast, creating alternatives and marshaling resources to achieve results; develop your "hustle muscle."

2. **Seek out incremental wins**—instead of immediately revolutionizing the company, start small and crush a few things first; once you've earned trust, you will garner bigger responsibilities and influence.

3. **Defend organizational change**—inevitable resistance can be mitigated if the change is carefully discussed, planned, embraced, communicated and ultimately defended.

"The truth is, no matter what your lifestyle or occupation, nothing can really stop you when you're allowing yourself to be exactly who you want to be."

HAYLEY WILLIAMS (PARAMORE)

NEVER STOP PLAYING YOUR PART

BEING A LEADER in a business culture that rocks is a massive undertaking, but it garners epic, long-term results. In fact, performance-oriented cultures possess statistically better financial results. For culturally strong brands like Whole Foods, In-N-Out Burger, LEGO or Walt Disney World, there is no doubt about the validity of their results in almost every area. Employee morale is higher and turnover is lower than their industry norms. People are passionately and actively engaged in the business. And because of these internal factors, organizational alignment filters through the entire brand, all focused on collectively achieving the company's goals, including the all-important financial ones. What starts out as an internal approach becomes external, profitable and sustainable results.

As brilliant business guru Seth Godin once stated: "Powerful organizations and great brands got there by aligning with and accelerating tectonic cultural shifts, not by tweaking sales one at a time."

Since we know that organizational cultures can only be affected by people and their behaviors, it should be clear that everything starts and ends with leadership. Regardless of position, any leader can enhance a company's environment, so never stop playing your part to advocate for and drive the culture.

Let's look at some ways to do that, starting with getting everyone to sing off the same sheet of music.

TEAM ALIGNMENT

In every way, culture matters. And yet, some leaders just don't get it. They do not study or celebrate the financial successes of such vibrant brands as Peloton, Salesforce, BurgerFi or Coca-Cola or give any credit to their cultures. Their own style relies on muscling the results through standard processes and procedures, using threats, punishments and fear as performance incentives. If this mindset is pervasive in the leadership, confusion will spread throughout the organization.

If the masses see their company's culture in a certain way and a leader perceives it in another (or does not perceive it at all), the team will not be aligned and the organization's results could be at risk. Too often, a company's staff and managers internalize a crystal-clear vision of their brand's culture, while its top leaders maintain a blurred or unfavorable perception of it.

Ironically, these same top leaders may attribute their negative business results to an unhealthy organizational culture. They might not use those exact words, but they talk about the team's lack of will or a flawed process or clashing visions of the overall goal. However, as you by now are likely starting to get, if you fix the culture, you fix the company.

Culture monumentally influences both internal employee behaviors and external company performance. This is why leaders at all levels need to advocate for culture change and alignment across the organization.

Your brand's image is the most critical component of your company's competitive differentiation over time. Culture must be effectively nurtured by the people entrusted to keep it vibrant and sustainable. To use an example from the world of rock and roll: when the leader of a band is not supportive, it makes for frustration, conflict and ultimately long-term destruction.

Oasis | Rock Band

Noel Gallagher, of the rock group Oasis, attests to this when he recalls how his vision of the band's direction compared to the vision of his brother and lead singer, Liam. Their well-documented on-stage arguments and differing opinions were legendary. Liam, the band's founder and leader, constantly cursed and yelled at his brother and the other musicians and crew on stage, often during the middle of performances over even the smallest of issues.

I love Oasis. But I remember paying good money to see the band, only to have Liam go into a tirade and walk off stage before the show ended. The audience never got to hear the group's biggest hits, "Wonderwall" and "Champagne Supernova." What a disappointment. For a band that, in its early years, promised the world that it would be the next Beatles, this cultural conflict between the leader and the rest of the band was like poison. The disruptive internal personality conflict within Oasis ultimately led to the group's breakup in 2009. It took eighteen long years for the band to go from record-breaking phenom to disbandment, but through all its successes, Oasis was dying a slow death because of its unhealthy internal culture. It was death by a thousand cuts.

This happens all the time in organizations where the leaders and the rest of the company don't sing off the same sheet of music.

Even if your company is experiencing good times now, the business will eventually be at risk if the leadership culture is not strong or aligned.

THE BALANCE OF STYLES

If part of your role as a new or mid-level manager is getting everyone on the same song sheet, finding the right balance in your leadership style is another. Sometimes reservation and subtlety are required, and other times you have to act with fierce bravado. Although team members may prefer one style over the other, it's healthiest to strike an even tone and be able to draw on either quality.

I divide leadership styles into two buckets: internal and external. The internal style is one of a quiet deliberator, where you listen to and learn from others before acting. The external style is to boldly inspire greatness in others to act. It's like going from Billie Eilish to Billy Idol, from powerfully restrained to cut loose. There's a time to be humble and a time to "bring the thunder." And both are equally effective, if used the right way in the right moment. So, let's look at both styles.

HUMILITY

Humility can play a big part in driving culture and moving the company forward. But why is that important and what does it mean for a leader to be humble? In the simplest definition I've come across, megachurch pastor Rick Warren writes this about humility in *The Purpose Driven Life*: "To be humble is not to think less of oneself, but to think of oneself less."

Sometimes humility gets a bad rap. People see it as a weakness. But I see it as a leadership strength. Humble people can be so competent and confident in themselves that they don't feel the need to boast; rather, they let their actions speak for themselves and realize the power in empowering others.

THERE'S A TIME TO BE HUMBLE AND A TIME TO "BRING THE THUNDER."

———

Dr. Deborah Birx | Global Health Official

World-renowned global health official and medical expert Dr. Deborah Birx is a humble leader. Her professionalism, management skills and leadership style served Dr. Birx well throughout her career, having attained the levels of colonel, ambassador, U.S. global AIDS coordinator and, finally, coordinator of the White House's Coronavirus Task Force during the hot mess that was 2020.

Even though she previously held critical and stressful positions at the Department of Defense, National Institute of Health, Walter Reed Army Medical Center and the Center for Disease Control, I'm not sure anything could have prepared Ambassador Birx for the stress that came with the daily barrage of COVID-19 questions from the press, health officials, business owners, teachers and parents. Yet, Dr. Birx's superior technical expertise, combined with an inspiring passion and calm demeanor, endeared her to the nation and garnered big-time respect. Her humility was her strength. Even when she was out of favor with President Trump for publicly presenting data that was contradictory to his stance, Dr. Birx's forty-year reputation as a humble leader was secure. And refreshing.

Ken Pendery | First Watch

First Watch: The Daytime Cafe is the fastest-growing breakfast chain in the United States. Co-founder and chairperson emeritus Ken Pendery is also a humble leader—and the entire organization loves him for that. In fact, I have not met an executive or manager in the organization who does not credit Ken for shaping their own leadership growth while evolving the concept to a multimillion-dollar enterprise.

In the few consulting projects where I was lucky enough to be around Ken, I immediately noticed what his team was exposed to every day: quiet confidence, thoughtfulness, open-mindedness. Even though he is soft spoken, his team was motivated to follow him off the cliff—or, in this case, to own their competitive set. Which they do.

First Watch's current president and CEO, Chris Tomasso, an internally promoted executive disciple of Ken Pendery—who has seamlessly taken the brand to even greater heights—puts it this way when talking about Ken's leadership style: "Ken Pendery is a quiet, thoughtful leader who has earned the respect of the entire organization not only for his keen insights but for his kindness and his commitment to creating a culture that fosters personal and professional growth.

He is anything but weak and, in fact, can be very direct when it comes to pointing out things he sees during his very frequent restaurant visits. Still, he is never unprofessional and lives by the mantra 'just be nice.' First Watch has delivered industry-leading results year after year due to a culture of excellence that Ken established. Nobody wants to let him down. To me, there is nothing more powerful than a humble leader who is driven by a greater purpose. I feel fortunate to have had the opportunity to work alongside Ken Pendery for so many years."

Being humble helps to build trust and enable learning, which are critical in any environment— government or business. Humility may also seem counter-cultural to the rock star lifestyle that screams of swagger and spotlight, but there is great influence to those who have the grace to shine a light on others, give teammates the credit, volunteer to help, take accountability, seek out feedback, ask others for their opinion, truly listen to people without the intent to respond and (my favorite) be open to having their mind changed. A culture-driven leader like this would compel me to stick around for a long time.

BRING THE THUNDER

The external leadership style is about inspiring the masses, perhaps getting people to do the things that you want them to do that they might not have done on their own. That is one of my favorite definitions of leadership. You would like to think every employee on the team is ready to take the hill for you, but the reality is many need extra motivation. This is the time for some good old-fashioned leadership inspiration. It's time to bring the thunder!

Melissa Wiggins | Cannonball Kids' cancer Foundation

Melissa Wiggins' first-born son, Cannon, was diagnosed with stage IV neuroblastoma—a high-risk childhood cancer—when he was just twenty months old. Melissa and her husband, Michael, were told Cannon had a 50 percent chance of survival. During his year and a half of treatments, Melissa saw the horrific effects firsthand. The experience motivated her to spend hundreds of hours researching and learning about the enormous lack of funding and research dedicated to pediatric cancer and the effects that result from antiquated treatments, usually designed for adults. In 2014, Melissa and Michael Wiggins founded an

Orlando-based nonprofit, Cannonball Kids' cancer Foundation (CKc), with a mission to fund innovative research, better treatments and quality of life for children with cancer, and to educate for change.

Pediatric cancer remains the number-one killer by disease of children in the United States. Every day at least five children die from cancer or the side effects of the existing treatments. As many as 95 percent of childhood cancer survivors are likely to experience at least one late effect of treatment, with a third suffering life-threatening and chronic side effects. Clinical research has been slow to innovate because large, government-based grants are more often awarded to long-established researchers in the field. Because of Melissa's dedication and leadership, CKc has been transforming this landscape by funding innovative, first-of-its-kind research and educating the public on the realities of pediatric cancer.

From the time I was introduced to Melissa, via my business partner and author of *Black Sheep*, Brant Menswar—who also has a child dealing with a rare form of childhood cancer—I have been amazed by her inspirational leadership. Take a look at the many ways Melissa Wiggins brings the thunder:

- She implemented a rigorous, relationship-based, invite-only grant process, ensuring that 92 percent of CKc-funded trials are first of their kind in the U.S.

- In a few short years, she grew the internal organization to include supporters from around the world, parent volunteers and nationally recognized nonprofit executives.

- She worked with policy makers in Washington, D.C., to advance the effort to define and improve survivorship metrics of childhood cancer and secure more federal funding for it.

- Her leadership inspired volunteers in the community to create an annual fundraising Gold Gala that is attended by celebrities and thousands of supporters and donors, and produces millions of dollars for research funding.

- Her inspiration helped to create a national speakers bureau of more than sixty childhood cancer ambassadors to publicly teach and advocate for education, research and support.

When asked about Melissa's leadership, the executive director of CKc, Karen Neely Revels, said this: "Melissa is skilled at wading through the white noise to identify how the team can get the job done. Because of her passion and constant relationship building, when Melissa speaks, people listen. When someone tells her 'no,' Melissa hears, 'not right now.' Melissa knows her own strengths and enthusiastically incorporates people that can fill in the gaps on her team. Her leadership is one that empowers others. This was truly evident when she transitioned from executive director to volunteer in order for the organization to grow. Her unique style inspires others to follow."

Melissa Wiggins is a bona fide rock star and knows how to bring the thunder when it's needed. And in the world of pediatric cancer research, it's needed to move mountains.

As a leader, knowing which leadership style is required at any given moment is part of your role. Is it time for humility or bravado?

GREATEST HITS

1. **Align the team**—because employee behaviors collectively produce company results, you must understand, advocate for and communicate a clear direction across the company; get everyone singing off the same song sheet.

2. **Practice humility**—shine a light on others, give teammates the credit, volunteer to help, take accountability, seek out feedback, ask others for their opinion, truly listen to people and be open to having your mind changed.

3. **Bring the thunder**—some situations require extra inspiration and motivation to influence others; during those moments, act with fierce bravado.

"Pick your role models wisely; find out what they did and do it."

LANA DEL REY

MENTORSHIP IS INSTRU- MENTAL

ONE WAY to affect culture change is through personally developing others and being willing to be developed by others. So, humility is important here as well.

You are who you are today because of learned behavior, so humility may be one of those elusive leadership characteristics that takes a lifetime to embrace, especially if it is not part of your natural disposition. But if the selfless and humble side of you authentically exists, then you are ready for the next step. Mentorship is perhaps the greatest level of leadership maturity there is. And if mentorship is or becomes a widely celebrated part of your organization's learning environment, you can expect an army of culture catalysts to positively push the brand to new heights.

THE STIGMA OF ASKING

I remember hearing the word "mentor" early in my management career and being both confused about what it was and turned off by what it implied. Once I learned that specific people could help me with my leadership skills and career succession, you would think the analytical, academic side of me would have embraced any available guru. But the emotional, confident side of me thought: "Why do I need to seek advice from others? I made it to this level on my own. Why would I show any leadership weakness by asking others for help? I can figure things out myself."

I'm sure I wasn't alone in this mentality. The formal mentor programs in my company did not have the stickiness to last, nor did I see any great role model programs in the industry. I just assumed that the initial stigma I felt about mentorship was prevalent in most leaders. But I was wrong. Most business leaders today will gladly and publicly acknowledge the mentors that contributed to their success. As Facebook COO Sheryl Sandberg, author of *Lean In*, once said: "I feel really grateful to the people who encouraged me and helped me develop."

MENTORSHIP IS THE GREATEST LEVEL OF LEADERSHIP MATURITY THERE IS.

Mentors are trusted advisers and role models who traditionally have more experience than you in a specific area and willingly offer up perspectives, ideas, suggestions and wisdom to develop your leadership skills. They can be invaluable. If you develop a strong relationship with the right mentor, their wise counsel can help you withstand any challenges that arise— team dysfunction, economic recession, global pandemic and even job loss. They can be a shining light in the darkness.

Take the advice of *Shark Tank* entrepreneur and brand icon Daymond John, who said: "Align yourself with the right people, forge the right relationships and you'll set yourself up for the long run."

Mike Kneidinger | Hard Rock Cafe

Once I understood the value of mentors in my life, especially when I needed to compensate for some of my weaker leadership traits, I took full advantage. One of my role models was Mike Kneidinger, the former vice president of operations and COO for Hard Rock Cafe.

Mike Kneidinger's brilliance, passion and commitment led to his multiple promotions, including running all cafe operations in the franchise community and eventually the company-owned businesses. He was the right person at the right time to help the brand soar to iconic heights—producing year-on-year record financial results (and the greatest bonus checks I had ever seen).

MK, as we all came to know him, joined Hard Rock Cafe as the first externally hired general manager, practically taboo at the time. All others had previously been internally promoted. I was lucky enough to be Mike's first trainer during his management-in-training tenure in my home location, which kicked off a decades-long friendship and also an informal mentor/mentee relationship that helped develop me into the type of person I am now.

Here are some tentpole moments in our working relationship:

- When I planned out content and topics for our corporate university, instructional videos and e-learning courses, Mike was there as a guiding voice to ensure my team produced training that was needed and would be accepted in the field.

- When I decided to pivot in my training and development career, Mike encouraged me to put the plan together, take the risk and make the case.

- When I decided to start my own consulting company, Mike's sage advice helped me first craft and build a successful business, and then get out of that business when my heart just wasn't in it.

- When I struggled to understand why my marriage was failing, Mike consoled me and also challenged me about how I could handle it, his own experience being critical to our discussions.

- I even see MK's influence today in my professional keynote speaking. My delivery style on stage tends to be a bit loud, fast and aggressive, reminiscent of Mike addressing a group of restaurant GMs; perhaps that was more osmosis than formal discussion, but an impact nonetheless.

I can honestly say that I would not be the type of leader, speaker or person I am today if not for Mike Kneidinger. Even now that he has retired as president of Yard House restaurants, I regularly seek his counsel.

Do you have someone like that in your world?

ONE IS NOT ENOUGH

Perhaps you are lucky enough to have more than one mentor. In fact, most experts say you ought to have at least two—one inside your company to seek comprehensive advice on known issues and one outside the organization as an objective, third-party perspective. But I think you should have even more than that.

Anthony Tjan, business expert and author of *Good People*, thinks several mentors in a person's life will develop them in incredible ways. He puts it this way: "The best mentors can help us define and express our inner calling, but rarely can one person give you everything you need to grow."

Don Yaeger | Author, Speaker, Consultant

Don Yaeger, eleven-time *New York Times* bestselling author and long-time writer and editor for *Sports Illustrated*, calls it your "inner circle," a concept he learned from his mentor, the iconic late UCLA college basketball coach John Wooden. During one of their mentorship discussions, Wooden stressed to Don the importance of being intentional about who is in your inner circle. You only have so much emotional energy to give to others, so surround yourself with those that you trust, admire and respect enough to give you the advice you need to grow. Having a huge group of friends is great, but a council of four to five confidants who have a vested interest in your development is key.

Although there are many ideas on the exact number of mentors you could have in your inner circle, I have come to realize that the following five mentor types are the most important (and the easiest to remember):

- **Internal mentor**—this senior person traditionally works with you at the organization and has accumulated wisdom through years of experience; they can provide insight into the business, helping you fine-tune your leadership skills and advise you on big strategic decisions in your career.

- **External mentor**—this high achiever is outside your company but understands your industry and the role you play in it; they are a great resource when you need an unbiased perspective. This mentor can be considered a cheerleader for you, is an advocate for you and your work, and will talk you up to others. They can also be a resource connector, introducing you to useful people in your industry.

- **Peer mentor**—this is the colleague who can talk through projects with you, advise you in navigating certain personalities and listen to you vent over coffee. This type of mentoring relationship works best when it's reciprocal, as in peers committed to supporting each other, collaborating and holding each other accountable.

- **Personal mentor**—this is someone who gives you a psychological lift and helps you see light through the cracks during challenging times. They have your overall best interests in mind and can be particularly helpful in achieving work-life balance. This person doesn't have to work in your industry and could be a friend, a family member or a life partner.

- **Reverse mentor**—extremely underrated, this person could be the individual *you* are mentoring, even though they may have fewer years in the workplace than you. Talking with "mentees" gives you the opportunity to collect feedback on your leadership style, engage with a younger generation and keep your perspectives fresh and relevant.

Having a mentor to rely on is a great step in a leader's development, but having multiple sounding boards for different aspects of life—each a willing participant in your success—may be the epitome of humility and ultimate growth.

As you look at the five mentor types above, can you identify someone who plays a part in each of these roles? I'm sure I'm not the only one who has a trusted person in each, but I'm so thankful that I do.

THE CHOSEN ONES

The widely preferred method for mentoring programs within organizations seems to be creating a formal, structured program in which mentors are assigned to mentees, one to one. This requires some real planning to ensure all parties and the organization are served well. How the specific pairings are established, the length of time for the formalized relationship and the communication methods used all affect the quality of the program. Each of these factors comes with its own set of challenges, but many companies swear by their programs' successes.

However, if your company has no formal program, as a new leader you should seek to create your own "inner circle."

Don't wait to be reminded to focus on your own development.

Some experts say choosing your own mentors is a better approach, anyway, and it allows more freedom and flexibility. If you go this route, here are some things to consider when choosing a mentor:

- **Willingness**—ensure the person is willing to spend the time and energy to mentor you.

- **Value orientation**—make sure your values are aligned, so there are no fundamental issues in listening to or taking the mentor's advice.

- **Clear expectations**—set clear expectations on both sides, including about the frequency of connection, the communication methods, the work involved, the overall length of time of the "program" and confidentiality.

- **Style**—pay attention to the mentor's personality, especially when in leadership. If it is not role-model worthy, the chances of you amping up your own leadership are low.

It may not shock you to know that some of the world's best-known companies have a formal mentoring program in place, but I was taken aback to read in a 2019 *Forbes* article that over 70 percent of Fortune 500 companies have one in place and that 75 percent of executives credit their mentors with helping them reach their current positions.

Whoa. If that isn't an endorsement for mentoring, I don't know what is.

If securing some mentors and being one yourself are not already on your leadership list of things to do, let's get at it. It's too important for your career to ignore.

GREATEST HITS

1. **Embrace mentorship**—rely on others to assist you, provide feedback, challenge your thinking and celebrate you; this is one of the greatest growth paths for leaders.

2. **Create your inner circle**—identify four to five irreplaceable, intentional mentors in your life and formally develop those relationships; choose people who already have a vested interest in your success.

3. **Get with the program**—if you have access to a formalized company mentorship program, take full advantage of it; 70 percent of successful Fortune 500 companies can't be wrong.

"The cool thing about passion is that no matter how good or bad a day you're having, tomorrow's going to be better because passion finds some way of doubling itself."

GARTH BROOKS

LIGHT IT UP

WHEN I discuss culture with business leaders, most of our conversations center around the desire to enhance their company's culture, but a fortunate few get to experience a brand during its inception, when it comes blazing out of the starting gate with a strong culture. A rock star workplace developed because a careful founder or business owner fueled the initial cultural flame of the organization.

THINK LIKE A FOUNDER

By definition, a person who starts an organization should be considered a catalyst. To create a culture so crystal clear that the company's "personality" is apparent to all requires deliberate thought, strategy and action. Such business leaders recognize the staying power of a strong brand personality; they aspire to positively ingrain the brand's culture into the end user's psyche—from "genesis" to "nirvana."

Perhaps one day, you will start your own business, but even if your current role is a new up-and-coming leader or middle manager, you should still think like a founder. We can learn a lot from them.

Scott and Ally Svenson | MOD Pizza

One of my favorite company cultures is MOD Pizza, with MOD standing for "made on demand." Co-founders Scott and Ally Svenson revolutionized the traditional pizza industry by creating the first super-fast pizza concept.

After starting and selling two incredibly successful coffee concepts—Seattle Coffee Company and Carluccio's Caffè—the Svensons opened the first MOD Pizza in 2008, and the "pizza with a purpose" brand skyrocketed. Known for its artisan-style pizzas that are individually sized, made on demand, completely customizable and ready in minutes, MOD Pizza is a people-first company culture like no other. At the heart of the business is the idea that if Ally and Scott take care of their employees (the MOD Squad), they'll take care of the customers, and the business will take care of itself. It's the old "service profit chain" model known throughout the restaurant industry, but the Svensons call it "Spreading MODness." And it works.

By putting people first, the founders strive to be a force for positive change in the lives of MOD Squadders and the communities they serve. From paying above-industry rates and offering benefits, to hiring unique people who would not get a second look elsewhere, the company is deeply rooted in acceptance, opportunity and development. The result? A culture of loyal brand ambassadors who give customers mind-searing experiences.

One heart-centered way the Svensons fuel the company's cultural flame is by employing "impact hires," or three types of employees that MOD aspires to bring on board at every location:

- **Opportunity youth**—young adults aged eighteen to twenty-four who are severely under-employed and statistically likely to live a life of crime if not given a chance to work

- **Second chances**—primarily people who have been convicted of a crime and have spent time in jail or prison

- **People with disabilities**

Opening up hundreds of new locations each year, MOD Pizza has been named the fastest-growing restaurant chain in the U.S. for several years (Technomic, *Nation's Restaurant News*) and recently named "most loved brand" by Foodable. As good as the pizza and the concept is, the innovative culture that Scott and Ally Svenson created is what truly ignited my business crush on the brand. Having previously invested in a fast-casual pizza business myself, I can assure you that MOD Pizza was always the role model and the envy of the industry. The founders knew exactly what the world needed—and it wasn't just a stellar pie.

Gretchen Bauer | BSWANKY

"Not all workplaces are created equal," says Gretchen Bauer, founder and CEO of BSWANKY, a trailblazing luxury handbag manufacturer in Sarasota, Florida. Bauer's world was rocked when, while developing an interior design business, she received a tote bag made in a Florida-based factory where the workers earned less than minimum wage. She subsequently visited several retail factories that had substandard working conditions. Particularly in the retail industry, women's factory labor is undervalued (including in the U.S.)

and takes place in less-than-optimal environments. Gretchen Bauer decided to create a totally different business around luxury handbags, but also to establish a work environment forged with integrity, creative expression and intention.

From its inception, BSWANKY was rooted in the purpose-driven goal that all roads lead to "being the difference." You only need to look at some of Bauer's leadership initiatives with the team to know this is true. She:

- hires an employee base made up almost entirely of immigrant women artisans;

- involves the artisans in the entire design process;

- encourages the team to scrutinize every detailed step in the process of producing an item, constantly considering the best interests of the customers and employees;

- supplies a custom-designed lounge, specifically for the employees to take breaks and eat lunch away from their machines;

- provides a weekly catered lunch of healthy food and smoothies;

- creates a four-day work week—you got it, all associates have Fridays off; and

- supports multiple philanthropic causes, including charities that address hunger, breast cancer, mental illness, medical supplies and Latina entrepreneurs.

Can you envision the fun work environment these women must have with lively music playing in the foreground, a facility stocked with fruit, fancy waters and healthy snacks, flexible work schedules, fun lunches and free educational opportunities—all centered around work with a purpose? It's amazing.

Gretchen Bauer and Scott and Ally Svenson created their unique cultures from the ground up. Shepherding a great culture into the world is a tough thing, but the responsibility of caring for and maintaining it can also be quite daunting for a new leader. Like the entrepreneur who started the company in the first place, every leader in the brand must take great care to ensure the business' viability—both financial *and* cultural. To do this, you have to constantly think like a founder—consider your bigger mission, innovate and take actions to light up the hearts of your people and your customers.

KEEP THE FIRE BURNING

As important as it is to spark the flame of a company's culture, it's just as critical to keep the fire burning. Most new leaders start off in an existing culture. They didn't create it. Instead, they have the awesome responsibility of being flag bearers of a founder's vision. Like me when I joined Hard Rock Cafe in 1991, you may have inherited a great culture that needs to be perpetuated for the future. Regardless of the state of the culture, on a scale of one to ten (and with a proper nod to Spinal Tap), your goal as a leader is to "take it to eleven."

Brian Moynihan | Bank of America

Brian Moynihan, the chair and CEO of Bank of America, leads a team of 210,000 employees dedicated to making financial lives better for people, companies and institutions around the world. The reignition of the megabank's culture began with the steady leadership era of Brian Moynihan.

Moynihan's first decade in the top leadership role was bracketed with crisis. He took over in 2010, having been dealt a global financial crisis, only to ride into his tenth year facing a global health crisis. Yet, during those complicated and turbulent times, Moynihan positioned the company to be a stable industry leader. Check out just a few of the initiatives Brian Moynihan implemented during his initial tenure, which may telegraph a lot about his leadership style and the culture of the business:

- The lowest-paid associates receive a minimum pay rate of $20 per hour.

- Employee surveys are conducted annually, regardless of crisis or the health of the organization.

- Staff are encouraged to take the day off on Juneteenth to commemorate the end of slavery in the U.S.

- The company has committed $300 billion over the next decade to environmentally friendly businesses.

Four bullet points. That's it. I could have listed so many more, but these in particular highlight the breadth of Moynihan's leadership in stoking the cultural flame of the brand in a variety of areas.

Arne Sorenson, president and CEO of Marriott International, says of Moynihan: "Through thick and thin and thin again, Brian Moynihan has led Bank of America with humility and a focus on the long term, delivering extraordinary results and strong team spirit."

Because of Moynihan's leadership, BOA has won several top awards and recognition for best workplaces for diversity, women, parents and disability inclusion. To round out his first decade, *Chief Executive* magazine selected Brian Moynihan as their 2020 CEO of the Year—previous winners include Bill Gates, Jack Welch, Herb Kelleher and Bob Iger. Now, that's a great list of rock star business leaders.

With the daunting task of leading the organization during the COVID-19 pandemic, Moynihan stuck to his principles of employees first. Where some companies furloughed or terminated staff, Moynihan refused to cut into BOA's greatest asset: its talent. Instead, he doubled down on the team, knowing that their health and well-being would serve the clients well during that unprecedented time. Take a look at the amazing initiatives Bank of America implemented once the crisis seemed imminent, which only further validates Moynihan's CEO of the Year award. The bank:

- assigned more than 10,000 people to work on quickly getting loans and funds support to customers in need;

- doubled the amount of overtime pay for call centers to ensure clients were serviced and the system never slowed down;

- provided associates working from home with equipment to be effective from a distance;

- gave team members the unlimited ability to talk to a counselor, if they needed to;

- offered that employees could speak to a telemedicine doctor without paying a co-pay;

- provided lunch daily to all associates working in financial centers during the quarantine lockdown; and

- covered daycare costs (up to $100 per day) for any associate who needed someone to watch their children while working in a branch or office.

You may be thinking, "Sure, that's a massive financial institution with the funds to do all that … " but many similar companies that *could* have did not. That's the point. Brian Moynihan is a courageous leader. He continues to reignite the cultural flame of his company in almost every area.

LEADERS HAVE THE POWER TO LIGHT UP OR EXTINGUISH THE CULTURAL FLAME OF A COMPANY.

———

FIND THE FLAMETHROWER

As a leader, you always have a choice about where to spend your time, energy, focus and funds. Regardless of your business, you will be defined by your leadership decisions. Especially during tough times of crisis.

Culturally strong companies like MOD Pizza, BSWANKY and Bank of America would not be where they are today without strong leadership: passionate, committed and thoughtful people who were determined to take their brand to rock icon status. The amazing positive results organizations produce do not happen because of some branding, a business program, an internal process or even the product itself—leadership creates that trajectory. Leaders make success happen. And it is crystal clear that leaders who focus on company culture as *the* means to an end light it up, reaping long-term rewards.

Leaders have the power to light up or extinguish the cultural flame of a company. Those who "get it" bring the flamethrower. Let's go light up the culture.

GREATEST HITS

1. **Own the place**—act as if you started (or own) the business; this will create added focus, commitment, inspiration and guidance to crafting the right culture (putting employees first, being intentional about giving back and so on).

2. **Light the fire**—an established culture needs to be catered to, amped up and perpetuated for the future. Regardless of the state of the culture, take it to eleven.

3. **Be the accelerant**—you have the power to light up the cultural flame of the company. It's not going to happen because of programs, processes, tools, branding or the product itself; focus on the culture and light it up.

ENCORE

A COMPANY'S CULTURE starts with strong, directed leadership. This is true whether the culture is to be created, maintained, adjusted or completely reimagined. Harkening back to my earlier definition, a company culture is initially created by a collection of individual behaviors. So, whether or not they purposefully seek to affect the organization's culture, leaders, by nature of their position, will do so with their actions or inactions. This leadership effect can have positive (or negative) consequences for the brand's culture.

Small businesses and large corporations alike reap huge rewards from a great company culture.

BENEFITS OF A STRONG CULTURE

Here are some of the unmistakable benefits that come from leaders igniting the cultural flame of the brand:

- **You attract rock stars**—intentionally creating a strong work environment makes others want to join the band. Hiring rock star talent (versus lip-synchers) moves the company forward and attains results.

- **You increase employee retention**—the cost of losing an employee is a huge financial drag on the business. When team members are excited about their daily responsibilities, they are less likely to leave for another job. Developing a great culture will influence employees to stick around longer.

- **You enhance productivity**—when employees are happy, they consistently show up, take fewer sick days and stay engaged in the work, giving 100 percent effort while they are there.

- **You generate more revenue**—as happy customers continue to immerse themselves in an awesome company culture (based on employee behaviors), they will become loyal to your organization, not only spending more money on your products and services but becoming brand advocates and referring others to you.

- **You improve brand reputation**—the way your community views your company has the power to catapult you to higher sales, more and bigger donations, more media impressions and so on, ultimately creating a positive buzz about your business. That keeps customers coming back.

- **You strengthen the bottom line**—this is the ultimate metric in most businesses: the bottom line of a profit and loss statement. Even in nonprofit volunteer organizations, a focus on the bottom line is critical. Combining all the cultural benefits I listed above will result in more profit for the brand. Gone are the days when this financial byproduct of a great company culture is considered a myth.

Time to Show Up

Focusing on the company's culture may be new to you, but the benefits are herculean. Building a strong culture creates an enjoyable, encouraging and inspiring work environment that everybody wants to be part of. Your brand will see undeniable benefits when you do it right. But talk and thought are cheap.

You have to put in the work to truly start your cultural revolution. It is not enough to just fondly think of these proven best practices from time to time and expect better results—you have to act. As *The West Wing* fictional TV president Jed Bartlet (played by Martin Sheen) famously said: "Decisions are made by those who show up."

It's time to show up.

NEXT STEPS

Here are some immediate initiatives you can do to enhance your leadership and get the fire going:

- **Proof the Greatest Hits**—as a holistic refresher, flip through this book again, paying particular attention to the "Greatest Hits" section at the end of each chapter.

"Decisions are
made by those
who show up."

JED BARTLET

- **Share the book**—distribute copies of *Leadership That Rocks* to your team, who can also be culture catalysts and collectively discuss how to amp up the brand.

- **Grab the workbook**—access the free *Leadership That Rocks* companion workbook at LeadershipThatRocksBook.com. The workbook requires some specific efforts on your part; it will serve as a customized deep dive into your leadership and a detailed project outline for next steps.

- **Take the assessment**—download the free Culture Assessment at CultureThatRocks.com. This will provide an introspective gut check on where you, your team and your brand are as a *culture that rocks*.

- **Listen to the podcast**—subscribe to *Thoughts That Rock*, the free weekly edu-taining leadership podcast that I co-host with Brant Menswar. We discuss life-changing pieces of advice with "rock star" guests.

- **Get the series**—read the other books in the Culture That Rocks series—*Service That Rocks* and *Engagement That Rocks*—to keep learning about the big focal points of an iconic culture.

- **Pitch external expertise**—you may not be the ultimate decision maker, but recommending new cultural material and outside-the-box thinking from an external source is a great way to affect change, while also getting noticed and advancing your career. (Psst... I happen to know a speaker or two who can deliver in-person or virtual sessions for this exact strategy.)

Leadership isn't easy. But as you often hear, nothing worthwhile ever is. Being the cultural custodian of a company that you love is an awesome responsibility and (to quote my friend Brant) requires a lot of "deliberate intention." I'm just so honored that you made *Leadership That Rocks* a part of your journey and a resource in providing you clear direction throughout your career.

It doesn't matter if you started with the business at its inception or walked into a legacy brand that needs an overhaul—you *can* make a difference. You *will* make a difference.

That's what *leaders that rock* do.

I can't wait to hear about your journey.

Rock On—

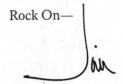

ACKNOWLEDGMENTS

BIG-TIME THANKS goes to the following family, friends and mentors who each supported me in some way along the journey to craft *Leadership That Rocks*: my mom and dad, Kathleen Wood, Toni Quist, Brant Menswar, Melissa Gillespie, Bobbie Gillespie, Daniel Botero, Chris Tomasso, Felicia White, Karen Neely Revels, Rebecca Sonkiss, Gretchen Bauer, Mike and Carol Shipley, Rich Johnson, Axum Coffee, Starbucks and the city of Winter Garden, Florida.

My sincerest gratitude goes to Page Two Books, who took a chance on me from day one and brought my vision to life. From the first discussion I had with Jesse Finkelstein to the ongoing guidance of the entire team, I always felt like I was in great hands. Gabi kept me organized, Tilman cleaned up my flaws, Peter made me look good and Chris and Madison helped me amplify my voice.

Finally, a huge thank you goes to Kendra Ward, my amazing editor at Page Two, who was a pure joy to work with. Kendra's personality and editorial style—the perfect balance between humility, patience, detail and expertise—helped me clarify my voice. Kendra is a rock star!

PRODUCTS

CULTURE THAT ROCKS
How to Revolutionize a
Company's Culture
2014

**LEADERSHIP
THAT ROCKS**
Take Your Brand's
Culture to Eleven and
Amp Up Results
2021

SERVICE THAT ROCKS
Create Unforgettable
Experiences and Turn
Customers into Fans
2022

ENGAGEMENT THAT ROCKS
Recruit and Retain
Chart-Topping Talent
2023

**LEADERSHIP THAT
ROCKS COMPANION
WORKBOOK**

CERTIFIED ROCK STAR
Leadership training

THOUGHTS THAT ROCK
Weekly leadership podcast

BOOKSTAR PR
Digital book marketing
assistance for authors

ABOUT THE AUTHOR

JIM KNIGHT is an award-winning training and development veteran and culture catalyst who speaks on a variety of interactive topics, including programs on organizational culture, differentiated service and rock star leadership. During Jim's twenty-one-year career with Hard Rock International, his creativity and success garnered his team several industry awards for cutting-edge print, video, e-learning and instructor-led concepts. He was also recognized by *Training* magazine as representing one of the Training Top 125 companies in the world, across all industries, and has since been featured in *Entrepreneur* magazine, *Inc.* magazine, *Forbes* magazine and Fox Small Business News.

With a music degree in Vocal Performance and Education, a six-year stint as a public middle school teacher and his two decades with the Hard Rock brand, Jim uses all of his experience and expertise—

as a keynote speaker, podcaster and author—to assist leaders of all levels and industries in developing their skills and amping up business results.

Jim released his widely praised first book, *Culture That Rocks*, in 2014. It is now in its second edition— and is the impetus for *Leadership That Rocks*, book one in the Culture That Rocks series.

Jim also discusses life-changing leadership advice and best practices with influential guests on *Thoughts That Rock,* the free weekly edu-taining podcast that he co-hosts with Brant Menswar.

To contact Jim Knight, you can reach him at:

LeadershipThatRocksBook.com

JimKnightSpeaker

@KnightSpeaker

CPSIA information can be obtained
at www.ICGtesting.com
Printed in the USA
BVHW031106120521
607042BV00007B/786

9 781774 580660